Janus

poems by

Esther Lim Palmer

Finishing Line Press
Georgetown, Kentucky

Janus

Copyright © 2020 by Esther Lim Palmer
ISBN 978-1-64662-239-9 First Edition
All rights reserved under International and Pan-American Copyright Conventions. No part of this book may be reproduced in any manner whatsoever without written permission from the publisher, except in the case of brief quotations embodied in critical articles and reviews.

ACKNOWLEDGMENTS

These poems first appeared, sometimes in slightly modified form, in the following literary journals:

Oberon: "Starlight"
The Hungry Chimera: "Sift"
White Wall Review: "First Fruits"

Publisher: Leah Maines
Editor: Christen Kincaid
Cover Art and Design: Dusan Arsenic
Author Photo: Aika Cardin

Printed in the USA on acid-free paper.
Order online: www.finishinglinepress.com
also available on amazon.com

Author inquiries and mail orders:
Finishing Line Press
P. O. Box 1626
Georgetown, Kentucky 40324
U. S. A.

Table of Contents

Sift 1

Starlight 2

Here, Away 3

Magic Hour 4

Ode To Olivia 5

Fairy Ring Eyes 6

The Master Jeweler's Daughter 7

Remembrance 8

Mister Nobody 9

Lingering 10

Hong Kong Expat 11

Broken Reflection 12

Somewhere Between 13

Burn 14

Wallflower 15

Love Chaos 16

I Like My Life 17

With You 18

Inclement 19

Breathe 20

First Fruits 21

Catching A Cloud 23

On Valencia 24

Opening Night 25

Too Much, Too Soon 26

Solitude 27

Less Than One 28

Crush 29

Korea 195X 30

*For
Olivia*

SIFT

Take my hand, before the sun
        sinks her magic, and bounded beauty
dissolves into a cool black cloak.
            There is no romance in the night—

only scattered static:
        "but this…" and "if only that…,"
clawing, clutching, for more noise:
        "why did he…?" and "why should I…?"

Brain locked beast! The sun will only rise
        to rescue another desperate dawn,
until the hourglass fixes her foot;
        then Time is no longer our friend.

So when the sand is warm,
        let us stay awhile.
And sift the grains, together;
        surely, they will silently slip through our fingers

if we let them?
        One sprinkling,
and then another.
        Over, and again.

Discard the damp, decaying, and damaged shells
        that pierce our pointed fingers
when we scour for answers alone,
        in bleak, and bleary-eyed darkness.

STARLIGHT

An empty glass rests
at the edge
of a tired game—
worn corners, and a missing dice.

She pulls the wool, wrinkled,
and creased, up to her eyes,
and begs the flame
to tell a tale:

the one that crackled pine cones,
and sucked them in—closer,
until their eyes watered,
and their cheeks flushed red;

days when marshmallows burned,
and chocolate melted—licked
off fingertips
that are now mostly ghostly white.

She lets the smoke sit in her hair—
the way it used to,
when they stayed in circles
only broken

to be outside:
knee-deep in snow,
heads tilted up, and slack-jawed,
by starlight.

HERE, AWAY

Find me here,
away
from the skyline of lights
that shines like fool's gold;
where Rumor rattles those
greedy streets
while hollow pipes play
for open ears
unstuffed of sense,
and grown men gorge
at discordant feasts—
rich in false comforts.
For how long
might I stay away?

Find me here,
still lingering here,
on this good old stump,
on that green grass hill;
where an easy breeze
gathers invisible songs,
and the sky softly glows
as the mighty sun bides
just below the line. And
hushed are those echoes
that encroach upon time.
Here, now. Hear, now,
a swarm of hope—
a rising hum.

MAGIC HOUR

Drift, would you?
With me?
Down
the crystal stream
that shimmers
over stones, and stroke
by stroke cleans
clear the dust
that gathers
between our toes,
as we bound
bare foot
by magic
hour,
through rambling
bridal white wild
flowers to hurry here—
here, to this hush-hush
stream—
to dip
and dip,
to wade. Wherever
the warm current
takes us:
we'll trust its clarity,
we'll trust its purity;
we'll trust it, naturally.

ODE TO OLIVIA

Beautiful babe, drifts off and away,
        with dreamland fairies, she flies,
though swaddled in a fountain of flowers—
        father's lips, mother's eyes.

Home in my arms, so close to my heart
        that beats to her breath's ebb and flow.
Notice her hair, watch it sway in the wind,
        her smiles, they come, they go.

Dusty degrees adorn closed doors,
        she flipped to switch my course.
Trophies, jewels, and treasure chests,
        abandoned, with little remorse.

Embark on explorations anew,
        heed my heart, I'll trace her lead.
Valleys, meadows, over mountaintops—
        gallop (O, sunshine!), my sovereign steed!

FAIRY RING EYES

I happened upon a kingdom, wise,
        where royalty bowed graciously;
hands low and lean were offered to me—
        billowing beams of gold.

I climbed a coat of bare bronzed bark,
        to hot top needles that tickled palms.
I slung my hammock between its arms:
        yes, I slinked into a redwood for the night.

Shadows released by a sinking sun,
        as cool swirls nudged, and warm lips lured;
mystical mists in patchwork lulled
        the kingdom, my keeper, and me.

So splendid was this regal realm,
        discrete with my sweet slumber,
'til dawn's new light, with its soft breeze,
        whispered, wakened me.

"We make no claim to know all truths,
        but, to be? There is no question:
a gift it is to breathe, to bleed,
        to inquire, to dare, to dream."

"We feel no fear of kingdoms dark,
        suckling sprouts after life, intertwined;
all rise, fully fledged, never melting—
        family of fairy ring eyes."

THE MASTER JEWELER'S DAUGHTER

When I peer into my pick of jewels,
        through glass in gilded frame,
I see perfection sparkling,
        imprinted, with your name.

Release the latch, locate once more,
        release my tended tear—
a happy tear, your gift to me;
        you hugged, and held me near.

Beauty does run deeper,
        for, in truth, one cannot see,
why I'm soldered to my locket,
        why it shines (just so) for me:

filled with fire, sleepless night,
        drab slab of gold, you took,
you plied, you polished, gave it life,
        a deep exhale, it shook.

"Open it," you urged, you beamed:
        it was you, and your love, in youth—
both bright-eyed and hopeful then,
        timeless goodness, truth.

Bodies, photos, memories, fade,
        yet my tear will drop, immortal—
you, for my daughter, and her daughters, to touch,
        when we poof, in a puff, with no portal.

REMEMBRANCE

The leaves that remain
are all yellow, like my face
before fading to white—waxy
half-moon at the margins
of a nothing night; waiting
only to wane, and then wane.
Was there a time before blank walls,
brittle bones, and this silent solitude?
Then all at once you recur
to me, having entered through
the window? Or the door?
Yes, here you are, as you always are
able to color my darkness
with tales of times when we danced
so dizzy in fields of flowers
for hours and hours; and I feel
the forgotten grass that tickled
our hems at the warm sun's insistence,
as we laughed aloud, and loved aloud.
And I remember, how we lived
with love and laughter.

MISTER NOBODY

his status was once
lost in desert,
many moons ago.
i tried to find him
the other day—
disconnected

perhaps, lost to us forever,
having found freedom
in anonymity—
mister nobody to others;
all things
to himself.
could you imagine
such lonely liberty?

i wonder, uncorking
another bottle, recalling
baklava we shared, so sweet;
wander, between
shifting sands and Sirius
and slink
        away
                to sleep.

LINGERING

Where no light shines, I lay awake
blind until shadows appear.
They do not move but watch and wait—
listening, for my soul to speak.

But my timid tongue
holds no great truths;
all mystery on mystery.
Only why, and what for?

So soon they too grow tired,
and leave me lonely to be—still empty
and lingering to know,
in darkness, yearning to see.

HONG KONG EXPAT

Bright lights! You blind the filthy rich,
who breathe to blow and binge.
Slur through choking smoke—inhale,
in blackened blur they singe.

Yet I am purely passing by,
a red-eye through the night.
Observer from the mountaintop,
giddy with green delight.

Oh fine, I'll buzz with blanc de blancs,
but this life is not for me.
Old leopard skin lady of *Lan Kwai Fong*,
no, nothing is for free.

All right, I'll stay for one more clink,
this is my favorite song.
And in a blink, the lights grow dim,
I'm emptied—
lost north for far too long.

BROKEN REFLECTION

At twenty-one,
        she's perplexed by married people.
 "To independence and empowerment!,"
she proclaims to her friends,
        sipping her cool, peach bellini.

At twenty-seven,
        she pities pregnant women.
"I'll never park my career; park myself,"
she confides in her sister,
        peeling off her pumps, and tailored suit.

At thirty-nine,
        she's a married, stay-at-home-mother.
"Who are you?,"
she whispers to her reflection,
        slipping into her tepid bath. Naked.

SOMEWHERE BETWEEN

Somewhere between fooling with fiction,
    and denying a dream.

Somewhere between waiting to wither,
    and racing to feel alive.

Somewhere between misplacing myself,
    and piecing together, the puzzle, that is me.

Will I always be
    somewhere between?

BURN

Round and around, sweeps the hand
on the clock; revolutions, resolutions, repeat.

Oh, but we were beautiful once!
Turgid, with two drops of dew;

now flaccid and sunken—the circle of ayes,
we're broken by popular pain,

and stained is the lens of our lives.
Dare I face my reflection? Who am I?

I am woman: a mother (fierce protector),
a sister, a fighter, a friend;

pulled and torn, pushed and worn,
fabric now threadbare and frayed.

Heavy hats? Yes, I have many.
Still the sun seeps through, to scorch.

So I'll burn for the next generation,
and humanity, she'll hold high her torch.

WALLFLOWER

Said the wallflower to a man:
If I had legs to spread and arms to stretch;
If I could dress in fancy French lace,
And drown myself in jasmine scents, would you
Take me, and display me? Adore me
For a whimsical while? Like your broken bike
And yesterday's clothes?
I think, therefore,
I will never know.

LOVE CHAOS

Snake charmers, stray cats,
djellabas, torn jeans,
saffron, cumin,
couscous, tajines,
tealights, souks,
"Special price, my friend!
Anything, everything!"
Paths, with no end.

"For a moment, I thought I'd lost you."
Breathless, you squeeze my hand,
and rush me to a golden door, adorned
with an inscription I struggle to read.

"Welcome home," you say,
smiling down at me—
me looking back
(*back out there!*), for more.

I LIKE MY LIFE

This spread looks amazing!
Have you posted it yet?

Thank you,
no. (I'm, like, actually living my life).

WITH YOU

Six feet deep
and deeper still,
I'll dive to feel alive with you.
Down here, your eyes
watch and warm my body,
searching for signs—
quick cues
skimmed over on the surface:
thumbs up, down here
I am O.K.;
thumbs up, down here
I seem magnified in this world,
almost as unmissable to you
as you are always to me.
But eventually air runs out,
and up
and up
to reality we must go—
plucked like a pair
of plastic figurines
from a nowhere-to-hide fish tank,
lit by a fake light.
If only I could've held my breath
just a little longer,
I'd have stayed
to be alive
with you.

INCLEMENT

What storm was willed to drench my heart, now dry?
All done with keeping kisses that remind
me of tender times; silky sheets inclined
to forgive and say, "oh well," with a sigh.
To tell you I've forgotten is a lie;
for rain still pounds on palettes in my mind—
blues too dark to ease and clean memory blind;
the drip and drip of torture to the eye.
Perhaps, I am merely the blustering wind
that howls, wreaking havoc waiting for spring.
Perhaps, you are the tree you claim to be;
rooted in truth, you will never rescind
your promise to see through seasons that bring
the rain, wind, and (respite) sweet songs, of me.

BREATHE

If, by some special magic
        we are changed, and shoot into stars,
                what would we gaze upon?

Players of the world,
        tinkering down below—
                one dot, and then another;

locked in a furious loop,
        manic in their macrocosms
                (microcosmic minds),

until the end of the line,
        when they are tangled and twisted,
                disconnected and disappear.

Awaken! And break the spell!
        Breathe in, breathe out. And notice
                the air that skims our skin.

Carry that cloak of kindness
        for others, and ourselves.
                Find warmth in awareness

that we are all,
        always learning.
                For it is not too late.

Though Father Time keeps watch over us,
        on this day, he remains
                our friend.

FIRST FRUITS

A lemon tree, I bought
for anniversary five (wood,
that gifted life):
Dwarf Meyer Lemon—

to bear mandarin blended
lemons, I think? (mixed,
like us?) But I am no expert
re: trees.

"Little effort, it'll thrive—
loads o' lemons, you won't keep up!
Squeeze the juice, freeze it.
Cool lemonade, for when the heat kicks in":

that's what the tree expert said,
on the farm, that day—
the one that unearthed the tree,
and fixed it in a plastic pot,

so I could turn it, and turn it again—
to find its flaws (but I didn't know
what I was looking for)—
"no blights in sight," he finally offered,

narrowing his eyes,
"no pests sticking 'round neither."
And so I nodded, and hugged it home
with me, to you.

We tended to the tree, together.
We talked to the tree (even when
it wasn't listening)—
      daily, then weekly,
           monthly, then,
                  no more. We stopped caring

    to learn
            how much sunlight it needed,
                    how much water it thirsted, or
                            just longed, to be left alone.

Our lemon tree died, naked and dry,
and our ring tan lines disappeared,
so many sunsets ago.

A lemon tree, I've since bought
for myself—just because.
It bore its first fruits today.

CATCHING A CLOUD

I saw a pink cloud—it raced through the sky,
I tip-toed to catch it, as it passed me by.
"But what are you doing?" you inquired of me,
eyes narrowed, brows furrowed.
"That cloud! Can you see?"

"Which cloud? There are many, come back inside,
rest your sweet head, and lay by my side.
Your body's trembling, warm tea's all you need,
come, take my hand,
come, follow my lead."

I cannot go with you, say the tears in my eyes;
I love you (did love you), but grown gray to despise.
The wind blows between us, and slams shut the door.
I take one step, then another,
and we, are no more.

ON VALENCIA

Grab a busy bag of goodies, so sweet:
of honey,
of milk;
but no time for a seat.

Card? No, cash only.
Would you care to tip?
No please, no thank you,
drips from your lips.

Name for the order?
Celeste, force a smile;
revert to your phone,
scroll through nothing worthwhile.

Whoosh out the door,
to your bus or your lift;
a face in the crowd,
again you will drift.

OPENING NIGHT

Forward-facing eyes,
and outstretched arms,
one bare foot, in front of the other.

One misstep, and she will fall from up high,
where he left her (for her own good).

The audience will hush with horror,
in a flash, he will rush to catch her.
But will he be, too late?

Better not to fall, to fail.
Make no mistake, there are no illusions—

the ringmaster is a proud man.
No family of clowns,
despite their painted smiles.

TOO MUCH, TOO SOON

Homework for the week:
"fail on purpose,
and see that when you do,
the world keeps turning.
And everything is ok."

She thanks N.,
signs a check,
and steps out
into the brisk San Francisco dusk.

She kicks the homework
around in her head,
all the way home.
A tentative turn of the key
unlocks her front door.

She fumbles for her phone,
and cancels her recurring Tuesday appointment.
Another door closes
behind her.

SOLITUDE

Solitude, once whispered, my name;
    heard my tears,
    sensed my fears.

Inadequacy had struck me down;
    'twas you who found my feet.

Forever hungry, for your vacuous words;
    to see your practiced smile,
    is satisfaction, enough.

LESS THAN ONE

She thinks she is better spoken to from the grave
where no blustering wind postures through the streets
begging for an equally empty reply.
Where the only sound is a gasp that words
on a page speak to her as they do.

She cries those ugly sentimental tears as she feels
understood. And although the page asks nothing
in return, when this passive player is refueled
with faith, she is prompted to offer her fraction
to the world. All her fragments never equaling one.

CRUSH

Between lands of broken languages,
we are lashed by a savage sea,

cornered by capricious waves,
that crush and confuse,

tired of treading water,
of translating the tides.

And yet, sunrise to sunset,
we find strength to strive—

strive to do more,
than to simply survive.

KOREA 195X

"But how does it end?"
Pat my head, and pinch the flame,
"You'll know tomorrow," you say.

I close my eyes, and do not hear
them take you, in the night—
boots, struggle, door slaps shut,
                (dreadful darkness).

You didn't mean to break your promise,
Father, you will come back. Or else, I'll find you.
I need to know, how the story ends.

Esther Lim Palmer was born in Rose Bay, New South Wales. To fulfill her South Korean immigrant father's wishes, she studied law at the University of Sydney, and practiced in Big Law for over a decade in Sydney, Hong Kong, and California. Her work has appeared in various literary journals, including *White Wall Review, The Hungry Chimera,* and *Oberon's Seventeenth Annual Issue*—selected to be archived in the EBSCO Humanities' database for universities and cultural entities interested in contemporary literary work. She currently lives and writes in San Francisco.

www.ingramcontent.com/pod-product-compliance
Lightning Source LLC
LaVergne TN
LVHW041507070426
835507LV00012B/1385